A Garden of Verse

Illustrated by
BENJAMIN PERKINS

CAXTON EDITIONS

First published by Caxton Editions Ltd
16 Connaught Street
London W2 2AF

© Caxton Editions Ltd, 1998
© Benjamin Perkins (illustrations), 1998

ISBN 1 84067 017 7

Designed and conceived by Savitri Books Ltd
Anthology compiled by Caroline Taggart

And when old words die out on the
tongue, new melodies break forth
from the heart; and where the old
tracks are lost, new country is
revealed with its wonders.

Gitanjali, Rabindranath Tagore

I love all beauteous things,
I seek and adore them;
God hath no better praise,
And man in his hasty days
Is honoured for them.

I too will something make
And joy in the making;
Altho' to-morrow it seem
Like the empty words of a dream
Remembered on waking.

Robert Bridges

Oh! there the chestnuts, summer through,
Beside the river make for you
A tunnel of green gloom, and sleep
Deeply above...

Here tulips bloom as they are told;
Unkempt about those hedges blows
An English unofficial rose.

Rupert Brooke

He that is down needs fear no fall,
He that is low no pride.
He that is humble ever shall
Have God to be his guide.
I am content with what I have,
Little be it, or much:
And, Lord, contentment still I crave,
Because thou savest such.
Fulness to such, a burden is,
That go on pilgrimage,
Here little, and hereafter bliss,
Is best from age to age.

John Bunyan

❦

How sweet the name of Jesus sounds
In a believer's ear!
It soothes his sorrows, heals his wounds
And drives away his fear.

It makes the wounded spirit whole,
And calms the troubled breast;
'Tis manna to the hungry soul,
And to the weary, rest.

John Newton

Does the road wind uphill all the way?
Yes, to the very end.
Will the day's journey take the whole long day?
From morn to night, my friend.

But is there for the night a resting-place?
A roof for when the slow, dark hours begin.
May not the darkness hide it from my face?
You cannot miss that inn.

Shall I meet other wayfarers at night?
Those who have gone before.
Then must I knock, or call when just in sight?
They will not keep you standing at that door.

Shall I find comfort, travel-sore and weak?
Of labour you shall find the sum.
Will there be beds for me and all who seek?
Yea, beds for all who come.

Christina Rossetti

Though the long seasons seem to separate
Sower and reaper or deeds dreamed and done,
Yet when a man reaches the Ivory gate
Labour and life and seed and corn are one.

Because thou art the doer and the deed,
Because thou art the thinker and the thought,
Because thou art the helper and the need,
And the cold doubt that brings all things to nought.

Therefore in every gracious form and shape
The world's dear open secret shalt thou find,
From the One Beauty there is no escape
Nor from the sunshine of the Eternal mind.

The patient labourer, with guesses dim,
Follows this wisdom to its secret goal.
He knows all deeds and dreams exist in him,
And all men's God in every human soul.

Eva Gore-Booth

All things bright and beautiful,
　　All creatures great and small,
All things wise and wonderful,
　　The Lord God made them all...

The cold wind in the winter,
　　The pleasant summer sun,
The ripe fruits in the garden,
　　He made them every one.

Cecil Frances Alexander

The rainbow comes and goes,
And lovely is the rose,
Look round her when the heavens are bare,
Waters on a starry night
Are beautiful and fair;
The sunshine is a glorious birth:
　But yet I know, where'er I go,
That there hath passed away a glory from the earth.

William Wordsworth

The King of Love my shepherd is,
Whose goodness faileth never;
I nothing lack if I am his
And he is mine forever.

Where streams of living water flow
My ransom'd soul He leadeth,
And, where the verdant pastures grow,
With food celestial feedeth.

Perverse and foolish oft I stray'd,
And yet in love He sought me,
And on His shoulder gently laid,
And home, rejoicing, brought me.

In death's dark vale I fear no ill
With Thee, dear Lord, beside me;
Thy rod and staff my comfort still,
Thy Cross before to guide me.

Thou spread'st a table in my sight;
Thy unction grace bestoweth;
And oh, what transport of delight
From Thy pure chalice floweth!

And so through all the length of days
Thy goodness faileth never;
Good Shepherd, may I sing Thy praise,
Within Thy house for ever.

Henry Williams Baker

Happy is the heart that sings!
Thanking God for little things,
Finding courage where a hill
Lifts its everlasting will,
Saying, when the night is dark,
'Morning cometh, and the lark!'

Happy is the heart that knows
Close communion with the rose,
Taking pleasure in the way
God has clothed a summer day,
Saying, when the clouds complain,
'There's a rainbow in the rain.'

Vivian Yeiser Laramore

My God, how wonderful Thou art,
Thy majesty how bright,
How beautiful Thy mercy seat,
In depths of burning light!

How wonderful, how beautiful
The sight of Thee must be,
Thine endless wisdom, boundless power
And awful purity!

Yet I may love Thee too, O Lord,
Almighty as Thou art,
For Thou hath stoop'd to ask of me
The love of my poor heart.

No earthly father loves like Thee,
No mother, e'er so mild,
Bears and forbears as Thou hast done
With me Thy sinful child.

Frederick William Faber

Time and again men sow the seed
And time and again the clouds send rain
And time and again men plough the fields
And time and again other owners come
And time and again beggars will beg
And time and again givers will give
And time and again give new gifts
And time and again find new heavens.

Buddhist monks' song

Hidden deep in the heart of things,
Thou carest for growth and life:
the seed becomes shoot, the bud a blossom,
the flower becomes fruit.
Tired I slept on my idle bed
in the illusion that the work had an end.
In the morning I awoke to find
that my garden was full of flowers.

Rabindranath Tagore

Hail to thee, blithe spirit!
Bird thou never wert—
That from heaven or near it
Pourest thy full heart
In profuse strains of unpremeditated art.

Higher still and higher
From the earth thou springest,
Like a cloud of fire;
The blue deep thou wingest,
And singing still dost soar, and soaring ever singest.

In the golden lightning
Of the sunken sun,
O'er which clouds are brightening,
Thou dost float and run,
Like an unbodied joy whose race is just begun.

Teach me half the gladness
That thy brain must know;
Such harmonious madness
From my lips would flow,
The world should listen then, as I am listening now.

Percy Bysshe Shelley

Music, when soft voices die,
Vibrates in the memory;
Odours, when sweet violets sicken,
Live within the sense they quicken.

Rose leaves, when the rose is dead,
Are heaped for the beloved's bed;
And so thy thoughts, when thou art gone,
Love itself shall slumber on.

Percy Bysshe Shelley

The fountains mingle with the river,
And the rivers with the ocean;
The winds of heaven mix for ever
With a sweet emotion;
Nothing in the world is single;
All things, by a law divine,
In one another's being mingle.
Why not I with thine?

Percy Bysshe Shelley

O God, my strength and fortitude,
Of force I must love Thee;
Thou are my castle and defence
In my necessity;

My God, my rock in whom I trust,
The worker of my wealth,
My refuge, buckler, and my shield,
The horn of all my health.

The Lord descended from above,
And bowed the heavens on high:
And underneath his feet he cast
The darkness of the sky:

On Cherubim and Seraphim
Full royally He rode;
And on the wings of mighty winds
Came flying all abroad.

Psalm 18

Awake, my soul, and with the sun
Thy daily stage of duty run;
Shake off dull sloth, and joyful rise
To pay thy morning sacrifice.

Thy precious time, misspent, redeem;
Each present day thy last esteem;
Improve thy talent with due care;
For thy great day thyself prepare.

Let all thy converse be sincere;
Keep conscience as the noontide clear:
Think how all-seeing God surveys
Thy secret thoughts, thy words and ways.

Wake, and lift up thyself, my heart,
And with the angels bear thy part,
Who, all night long, unwearied sing
High praise to the eternal King.

Thomas Ken

Our blest Redeemer, ere He breathed
His tender last farewell,
A Guide, a Comforter bequeathed
With us to dwell.

He came sweet influence to impart,
A gracious willing Guest,
While He can find one humble heart
Wherein to rest.

And His that gentle voice we hear,
Soft as the breath of even,
That checks each thought, that calms each fear
And speaks of Heaven.

And every virtue we possess,
And every conquest won,
And every thought of holiness
Are His alone.

Spirit of purity and grace,
Our weakness, pitying, see:
O make our hearts Thy dwelling-place,
And worthier Thee.

O praise the Father; praise the Son;
Blest Spirit, praise to Thee;
All praise to God, the Three in One,
The One in Three.

Henriette Auber

Father and Lover of our souls!

Though darkly round Thine anger rolls,
Thy sunshine smiles beneath the gloom,
Thou seek'st to warn us, not confound,
Thy showers would pierce the harden'd ground,
And win it to give out its brightness and perfume.

Thou smil'st on us in wrath, and we,
E'en in remorse, would smile on Thee;
The tears that bathe our offer'd hearts,
We would not have them stain'd and dim,
But dropp'd from wings of seraphim,
All glowing with the light accepted Love imparts.

John Keble

Grow old along with me!
The best is yet to be,
The last of life, for which the first was made:
Our times are in His hand
Who said, 'A whole I planned,
'Youth shows but half; trust God; see all nor be afraid!'

Robert Browning

The little cares that fretted me, I lost them yesterday,
Among the fields above the sea; among the winds at play;
Among the lowing of the herds, the rustling of the trees;
Among the singing of the birds, the humming of
    the bees.
The foolish fears of what might chance, I threw them
    all away
Among the clover-scented grass; among the
    new-mown hay,
Among the husking of the corn, where drowsy
    poppies nod,
Where ill thoughts die and good are born,
Out in the field with God.

Elizabeth Barrett Browning

I go to prove my soul;
I see my way as birds their trackless way,
I shall arrive! What time, what circuit first,
I ask not; but unless God sends His hail
Or blinding fire-balls, sleet, or stifling snow,
In good time, in His good time, I shall arrive.
He guides me and the bird. In His good time.

Robert Browning

All are not taken; there are left behind
Living Beloveds, tender looks to bring
And make the daylight still a happy thing,
And tender voices, to make soft the wind:
But if it were not so – if I could find
No love in all the world for comforting,
Nor any path but hollowly did ring
Where 'dust to dust' the love from life disjoined,
And if, before those sepulchres unmoving
I stood alone, (as some forsaken lamb
Goes bleating up the moors in weary dearth,)
Crying, 'Where are ye, O my loved and loving?' –
I know a Voice would sound, 'Daughter, I am.
Can I suffice for Heaven and not for earth?'

Elizabeth Barrett Browning

Mine eyes have seen the glory of the coming of
   the Lord,
He is trampling out the vintage where the grapes of
   wrath are stored;
He hath loosed the fateful lightning of his terrible
   swift sword,
His truth is marching on.

He has sounded forth the trumpet that shall never call
   retreat,
He is sifting out the hearts of men before his
   judgement seat.
Oh, be swift, my soul, to answer him! be jubilant,
   my feet!
Our God is marching on.

In the beauty of the lilies Christ was born across
   the sea,
With a glory in his bosom that transfigures you
   and me;
As he died to make men holy, let us die to make
   men free,
While God is marching on.

Julia Ward Howe

Fame or integrity: which is more important?
Money or happiness: which is more valuable?
Success or failure: which is more destructive?

If you look to others for fulfilment,
you will never be truly fulfilled.
If your happiness depends on money,
you will never be happy with yourself.

Be content with what you have;
rejoice in the way things are.
When you realize there is nothing lacking,
the whole world belongs to you.

Tao Te Ching

She follows me about My House of Life
(This happy little ghost of my dead youth!)
She has no part in Time's relentless strife,
She keeps her old simplicity and truth
And laughs at grim mortality –
This deathless child that stays with me –
This happy little ghost of my dead youth!

My House of Life is weather-stained with years –
(O Child in Me, I wonder why you stay).
Its windows are bedimmed with rain of tears,
Its walls have lost their rose – its thatch is gray:
One after one its guests depart –
So dull a host is my old heart –
O Child in Me, I wonder why you stay!

For jealous Age, whose face I would forget,
Pulls the bright flower you gave me from my hair
And powders it with snow – and yet – and yet –
I love your dancing feet and jocund air,
And have no taste for caps of lace
To tie about my faded face:
I love to wear your flower in my hair!

O Child in Me, leave not My House of Clay
Until we pass together through its door!
When lights are out, and Life has gone away,
And we depart to come again no more,
We comrades, who have traveled far,
Will hail the twilight and the Star
And gladly pass together through the Door!

May Riley Smith

For years I sought the Many in the One,
I thought to find lost waves and broken rays,
The rainbow's faded colours in the sun –
The dawn and twilight of forgotten days.

But now I seek the One in every form,
Scorning no vision that a dewdrop holds,
The gentle Light that shines behind the storm,
The Dream that many a twilight hour enfolds.

Eva Gore-Booth

The stars that round the Sun of righteousness
In glorious order roll,
With harps for ever strung, ready to bless
God for each rescued soul,
Ye eagle spirits, that build in light divine,
Oh! think of us today,
Faint warblers of this earth, that would combine
Our trembling notes with your accepted lay.

Your amarant wreaths were earn'd; and homeward all,
Flush'd with victorious might,
Ye might have sped to keep high festival,
And revel in the light;
But meeting us, weak worldlings, on our way,
Tired ere the fight begun,
Ye turn'd to help us in th'unequal fray,
Remembering Whose we were, how dearly won;

Remembering Bethlehem and that glorious night
When ye, who used to soar
Diverse along all space in fiery flight
Came thronging to adore
Your God new-born and made a sinner's child;
As if the stars should leave
Their stations in the far ethereal wild,
And round the sun a radiant circle weave.

John Keble

I am bound by the old promise,
What can break that golden chain?
Not even the words that you have spoken
Or the sharpness of my pain:
Do you think because you fail me
And draw back your hand to-day,
That from out the heart I gave you
My strong love can fade away?
It will live! No eyes may see it;
In my soul it will lie deep,
Hidden from all; but I shall feel it
Often stirring in its sleep.
So remember that the Friendship
Which you now think poor and vain,
Will endure in hope and patience,
Till you ask for it again.

Adelaide Procter

Time was, I shrank from what was right
From fear of what was wrong;
I would not brave the sacred fight,
Because the foe was strong.
But now I cast that finer sense
And surer shame aside;
Such dread as sin was indolence,
Such aim at Heaven was pride!
So when my Saviour calls, I rise,
And calmly do my best;
Leaving to Him, with silent eyes
Of hope and fear, the rest.

John Henry Newman

Never believe the worst of a man
When once you have seen his best,
Of any loyalty worth the name
This is the surest test.

Gloria Storm, Nosmo King & Norman Longstaffe

Laugh, and the world laughs with you,
Weep, and you weep alone;
For this sad old earth must borrow its mirth,
It has trouble enough of its own.
Sing, and the hills will echo it:
Sigh, and it's lost on the air;
For they want full measure
Of all your pleasure,
But nobody wants your care.
Feast, and your halls are crowded,
Fast, and they'll pass you by;
Succeed and give,
And they'll let you live,
But fail – and they'll let you die.

Ella Wheeler Wilcox

The man of life upright,
Whose guiltless heart is free
From all dishonest deeds
Or thought of vanity:

The man whose silent days
In harmless joys are spent,
Whom hopes cannot delude,
Nor sorrow discontent:

That man needs neither towers
Nor armour for defence,
Nor secret vaults to fly
From thunder's violence.

He only can behold
With unaffrighted eyes
The horrors of the deep
And terrors of the skies.

Thus scorning all the cares
That fate or fortune brings,
He makes the heaven his book,
His wisdom heavenly things.

Good thoughts his only friends,
His wealth a well-spent age,
The earth his sober inn
And quiet pilgrimage.

Thomas Campion

Most glorious Lord of lyfe, that on this day,
Didst make thy triumph over death and sin:
And having harrowd hell, didst bring away
Captivity thence captive us to win:
This joyous day, deare Lord, with joy begin,
And grant that we, for whom thou diddest dye,
Being with thy deare blood clene washt from sin,
May live for ever in felicity.
And that thy love we weighing worthily,
May likewise love thee for the same againe:
And for thy sake that all lyke deare didst buy,
With love may one another entertayne.
So let us love, deare love, lyke as we ought,
Love is the lesson which the Lord us taught.

Edmund Spenser

Even such is Time, which takes in trust
Our youth, our joys, and all we have,
And pays us but with age and dust;
Who in the dark and silent grave,
When we have wandered all our ways,
Shuts up the story of our days:
And from which earth, and grave, and dust,
The Lord shall raise me up, I trust.

Walter Ralegh

Though Truth and Falsehood be
Near twins, yet Truth a little elder is.
Be busy to seek her; believe me this:
He's not of none, nor worst, that seeks the best.
To adore, or scorn, an image, or protest,
May all be bad. Doubt wisely; in strange way
To stand inquiring right is not to stray;
To sleep or run wrong is. On a huge hill,
Cragged and steep, Truth stands, and he that will
Reach her, about must and about must go,
And what the hill's suddenness resists, win so.

John Donne

Thou hast made me, and shall thy work decay?
Repair me now, for now mine end doth haste;
I run to death, and death meets me as fast,
And all my pleasures are like yesterday.
I dare not move my dim eyes any way;
Despair behind, and death before doth cast
Such terror, and my feebled flesh doth waste
By sin in it, which it towards hell doth weigh.
Only thou art above, and when towards thee
By thy leave I can look, I rise again;
But our old subtle foe so tempteth me
That not one hour I can myself sustain.
Thy grace may wing me to prevent his art,
And thou like adamant draw mine iron heart.

John Donne

When I consider how my light is spent,
Ere half my days, in this dark world and wide,
And that one talent which is death to hide
Lodged with me useless, though my soul more bent
To serve therewith my Maker, and present
My true account, lest he returning chide,
'Doth God exact day-labour, light denied?'
I fondly ask. But Patience, to prevent
That murmur, soon replies, 'God doth not need
Either man's work or his own gifts; who best
Bear his mild yoke, they serve him best. His state
Is kingly: thousands at his bidding speed,
And post o'er land and ocean without rest;
They also serve who only stand and wait.'

John Milton

Stone walls do not a prison make,
Nor iron bars a cage;
Minds innocent and quiet take
That for an hermitage;
If I have freedom in my love,
And in my soul am free;
Angels alone that soar above
Enjoy such liberty.

Richard Lovelace

Weep not, my friends! rather rejoice with me!
I shall not feel the pain, but shall be gone,
And you will have another friend in Heaven.
Then start not at the creaking of the door
Through which I pass. I see what lies beyond it!

Henry Wadsworth Longfellow

❧

There is no Death! What seems so is transition;
This life of mortal breath
Is but a suburb of the Life Elysian
Whose portal we call Death.
She is not dead – the child of our affection –
But gone unto that school,
Where she no longer needs our poor protection,
And Christ Himself doth rule.
In that great cloister's stillness and seclusion,
By guardian Angels led,
Safe from Temptation, safe from Sin's pollution,
She lives! whom we call dead.

Henry Wadsworth Longfellow

Nothing is so beautiful as Spring—
When weeds, in wheels, shoot long and lovely
  and lush;
Thrush's eggs look little low heavens, and thrush
Through the echoing timber does so rinse and wring
The ear, it strikes like lightnings to hear him sing;
The grassy peartree leaves and blooms, they brush
The descending blue; that blue is all in a rush
With richness; the racing lambs too have fair
  their fling.

What is all this juice and all this joy?
A strain of the earth's sweet being in the beginning
In Eden garden.—Have, get, before it cloy,

Before it cloud, Christ, lord, and sour with sinning,
Innocent mind and Mayday in girl and boy,
Most, O maid's child, thy choice and worthy the
  winning.

Gerard Manley Hopkins

Sweet bird! thy bow'r is ever green,
Thy sky is ever clear;
Thou hast no sorrow in thy song,
No winter in thy year!

John Logan

My heart leaps up when I behold
A rainbow in the sky:
So was it when my life began;
So is it now I am a man;
So be it when I shall grow old,
Or let me die!
The Child is father of the Man;
And I could wish my days to be
Bound each to each by natural piety.

William Wordsworth

How well the skilful gardener drew
Of flowers and herbs this dial new!
Where, from above, the milder sun
Does through a fragrant zodiac run:
And, as it works, the industrious bee
Computes its time as well as we,.
How could such sweet and wholesome hours
Be reckoned, but with herbs and flowers?

Andrew Marvell

Lessons sweet of spring returning,
Welcome to the thoughtful heart!
May I call ye sense or learning,
Instinct pure, or Heaven-taught art?
Be your title what it may,
Sweet the lengthening April day,
While with you the soul is free,
Ranging wild o'er hill and lea.

If, the quiet brooklet leaving,
Up the stony vale I wind,
Haply half in fancy grieving
For the shades I leave behind,
By the dusty wayside drear,
Nightingales with joyous cheer
Sing, my sadness to reprove,
Gladlier than in cultur'd grove.

Where the thickest boughs are twining
Of the greenest darkest tree,
There they plunge, the light declining—
All may hear, but none may see.
Fearless of the passing hoof,
Hardly will they fleet aloof;
So they live in modest ways,
Trust entire, and ceaseless praise.

John Keble

The Head that once was crown'd with thorns
Is crown'd with glory now:
A royal diadem adorns
The mighty Victor's Brow.

The highest place that Heav'n affords
Is His, is His by right,
The King of kings and Lord of lords,
And Heav'n's eternal Light.

The Joy of all who dwell above,
The Joy of all below,
To whom He manifests His love,
And grants His name to know.

The Cross He bore is life and health,
Though shame and death to Him;
His people's hope, His people's wealth,
Their everlasting theme.

Thomas Kelly

They are all gone into the world of light!
And I alone sit lingering here;
Their very memory is fair and bright,
And my sad thoughts doth clear. . .

And yet, as angels in some brighter dreams
Call to the soul, when man doth sleep;
So some strange thoughts transcend our wonted
  themes,
And into glory peep. . .

O Father of eternal life, and all
Created glories under thee!
Resume thy spirit from this world of thrall
Into true liberty.

Either disperse these mists, which blot and fill
My perspective still as they pass,
Or else remove me hence unto that hill,
Where I shall need no glass.

Henry Vaughan

He that is down needs fear no fall,
He that is low, no pride;
He that is humble ever shall
Have God to be his guide.

I am content with what I have,
Little be it or much;
And Lord, contentment still I crave,
Because thou savest such.

Fullness to such a burden is
That go on pilgrimage:
Here little, and hereafter bliss,
Is best from age to age.

John Bunyan

Were I (who to my cost already am)
One of those strange, prodigious creatures, man,
A spirit free to choose, for my own share,
What case of flesh and blood I pleased to wear,
I'd be a dog, a monkey, or a bear,
Or anything but that vain animal
Who is so proud of being rational.

John Wilmot, Earl of Rochester

O! never say that I was false of heart,
Though absence seemed my flame to qualify.
As easy might I from myself depart
As from my soul, which in thy breast doth lie:
That is my home of love; if I have ranged,
Like him that travels, I return again,
Just to the time, not with the time exchanged,
So that myself bring water for my stain.
Never believe, though in my nature reigned
All frailties that besiege all kinds of blood,
That it could so preposterously be stained,
To leave for nothing this wide universe I call,
Save thou, my rose; in it thou art my all.

William Shakespeare

Would you learn the road to Laughter-town,
O ye who have lost the way?
Would ye have young hearts though your heads
  be gray?
Go, learn from a little child each day,
Go, serve his wants, and play his play,
And catch the lilt of his laughter gay,
And following his dancing feet as they stray,
For he knows the road to Laughter-town,
O ye who have lost the way!

Kathleen Blake

Sweet words you utter,
And yet
What poisonous deeds!

Be quiet, O dear friend.
Let your actions speak
And then see
How all venom dissolves
Into nectar.

Kabir

"There is no God,' the wicked sath,
''And truly it's a blessing,
For what he might have done with us
It's better only guessing.'

'There is no God,' a youngster thinks,
'Or really, if there may be,
He surely didn't mean a man
Always to be a baby.'

'There is no God, or if there is,'
The tradesman thinks, ''twere funny
If he should take it ill in me
To make a little money.'

'Whether there be,' the rich man says,
'It matters very little,
For I and mine, thank somebody,
Are not in want of victual.'

Some others, also, to themselves
Who scarce so much as doubt it,
Think there is none, when they are well,
And do not think about it.

But country folks who live beneath
The shadow of the steeple;
The parson and the parson's wife,
And mostly married people;

Youths green and happy in first love,

So thankful for illusion;
And men caught out in what the world
Calls guilt, in first confusion;

And almost everyone when age,
Disease or sorrow strike him,
Inclines to think there is a God,
Or something very like him.

Arthur Hugh Clough

Who really knows, who could tell
Whence this creation flows, where is its origin?
With this great surge the gods appeared.
Who knows from where it arose?

This flow of creation, whence did it arise?
Whether it was ordered or was not,
He, the Observer in the highest heaven,
He alone knows, unless – He knows it not.

Rg Veda

..But sweeter yet than dream of Summer or
   Spring
Are Winter's sometime smiles, that seem to well
From infancy ineffable;
Her wandering, languorous gaze,
So unfamiliar, so without amaze,
On the elemental, chill adversity,
The uncomprehended rudeness; and her sigh
And solemn, gathering tear,
And look of exile from some great repose, the sphere
Of ether, moved by ether only, or
By something still more tranquil.

Coventry Patmore

The wave and the river are not two
But manifestations of one.
When it rises, it is water;
When it falls, it is water still!
Just because it is called a wave,
It does not cease to be water.

Kabir

Sweet dove! the softest, steadiest plume
In all the sunbright sky,
Brightening in ever-changeful bloom
As breezes change on high;

Sweet Leaf! the pledge of peace and mirth,
'Long sought and lately won,'
Bless'd increase of reviving Earth,
When first it felt the Sun;

Sweet Rainbow! pride of summer days,
Highset at Heaven's command,
Though into drear and dusky haze
Thou melt on either hand;

Dear tokens of a pardoning God,
We hail ye, one and all,
As when our fathers walk'd abroad
Freed from their twelvemonth's thrall.

How joyful from th'imprisoning ark
On the green earth they spring!
Not blither, after showers, the Lark
Mounts up with glistening wing.

John Keble

To Mercy, Pity, Peace and Love
All pray in their distress;
And to these virtues of delight
Return their thankfulness.

For Mercy, Pity, Peace and Love
Is God, our Father dear,
And Mercy, Pity, Peace and Love,
Is Man, His child and care.

For Mercy has a human heart,
Pity a human face,
And Love, the human form divine,
Love, Mercy, Pity, Peace.

Then every man, of every clime,
That prays in his distress,
Prays to the human form divine,
Love, Mercy, Pity, Peace.

And all must love the human form,
In heathen, Turk or Jew;
Where Mercy, Love and Pity dwell,
There God is dwelling too.

William Blake

Remember me when I am gone away,
Gone far away into the silent land;
When you can no more hold me by the hand,
Nor I half turn to go yet turning stay.
Remember me when no more day by day
You tell me of our future that you planned:
  Only remember me; you understand
It will be late to counsel then or pray.
Yet if you should forget me for a while
And afterwards remember, do not grieve:
  For if the darkness and corruption leave
A vestige of the thoughts that once I had,
Better by far you should forget and smile
Than that you should remember and be sad.

Christina Rossetti

He who bends to himself a joy
Does the wingèd life destroy;
But he who kisses the joy as it flies
Lives in eternity's sunrise.

William Blake

Dear thoughts are in my mind
And my soul soars enchanted,
As I hear the sweet lark sing
In the clear air of the day.
For a tender beaming smile
To my hope has been granted,
And tomorrow she shall hear
All my fond heart would say.

I shall tell her all my love,
All my soul's adoration;
And I think she will hear me
And will not say me nay.
It is this that fills my soul
With its joyous elation,
As I hear the sweet lark sing
In the clear air of the day.

Samuel Ferguson

In the greenest growth of the Maytime,
I rode where the woods were wet,
Between the dawn and the daytime,
The spring was glad that we met.

There was something the season wanted,
Though the ways and the woods smelt sweet;
The breath at your lips that panted,
The pulse of the grass at your feet.

You came, and the sun came after,
And the green grew golden above;
And the flag flowers lightened with laughter,
And the meadowsweet shook with love.

Algernon Charles Swinburne

It was not in the winter
Our loving lot was cast;
It was the time of roses -
We plucked them as we passed!

That churlish season never frowned
On early lovers yet:
O no - the world was newly crowned
With flowers when first we met!

Twas twilight, and I bade you go,
But still you held me fast;
It was the time of roses -
We plucked them as we passed!

Thomas Hood

The boast of heraldry, the pomp of power,
And all that beauty, all that wealth e'er gave,
Awaits alike the inevitable hour.
The paths of glory lead but to the grave.

Thomas Gray

A true seeker,
O Brother,
Is a rare being
Who listens
To the song
Of his soul –
Like a deer
Enchanted by the music
Of the hunter,
Oblivious to
The lurking death!

Kabir

On the wheel of time
Human life appears only rarely.
Rejoice as it lasts,
O Kabir!

A fruit once ripened
And fallen to the ground,
Can't be attached to the branch again.

Kabir

In the Principle Darkness hid darkness,
Undifferentiated surge was the whole world,
The pregnant point covered by the form matrix,
From conscious fervour, powerfully, brought forth the
One.

In the Principle, then, rose desire,
Which was the first seed of consciousness,
Then the wise, searching in their hearts, perceived
That in non-being lay the bond of being.

Rg Veda

Praise to the Holiest in the height,
And in the depth be praise;
In all his words most wonderful,
Most sure in all his ways.

John Henry Newman

Oh, is the water sweet and cool,
Gentle and brown, above the pool?
And laughs the immortal river still
Under the mill, under the mill?
Say, is there Beauty yet to find?
And Certainty? And Quiet kind?
Deep meadows yet, for to forget
The lies, and truth, and pain?. . . oh! yet
Stands the Church clock at ten to three?
And is there honey still for tea?

Rupert Brooke

Nothing, resting in its own completeness,
Can have worth or beauty; but alone
Because it leads and tends to farther sweetness
Fuller, higher, deeper, than its own.
Life is only bright when it proceedeth
Towards a truer, deeper Life above.
Human love is sweetest when it leadeth
To a more divine and perfect Love.

Adelaide Procter

Give a man a horse he can ride,
Give a man a boat he can sail;
And his rank and wealth, his strength and health
On sea nor shore shall fail.

Give a man a pipe he can smoke,
Give a man a book he can read:
And his home is bright with a calm delight,
Though the room be poor indeed.

Give a man a girl he can love,
As I, O my love, love thee;
And his heart is great with the pulse of Fate,
At home, on land, on sea.

James Thomson

A Book of Verses, underneath the Bough,
A Jug of Wine, a Loaf of Bread—and Thou
Beside me singing in the Wilderness—
O, Wilderness were Paradise enow!

Edward Fitzgerald

Of the bright things in earth and air
How little can the heart embrace!
Soft shades and gleaming lights are there –
I know it well, but cannot trace.

Mine eye unworthy seems to read
One page of Nature's beauteous book;
It lies before me, fair outspread –
I only cast a wishful look.

I cannot paint to Memory's eye
The scene, the glance I dearest love –
Unchanged themselves, in me they die,
Or faint, or false, their shadows prove.

In vain, with dull and tuneless ear,
I linger by soft Music's cell,
And in my heart of hearts would hear
What to her own she deigns to tell.

'Tis misty all, both sight and sound –
I only know 'tis fair and sweet –
'Tis wandering on enchanted ground
With dizzy brow and tottering feet.

But patience! there may come a time
When these dulls ears shall scan aright
Strains, that outring Earth's drowsy chime,
As Heaven outshines the taper's light.

John Keble

There is a book, who runs may read,
Which heavenly truth imparts,
And all the lore its scholars need,
Pure eyes and Christian hearts.

The works of God, above, below,
Within us and around,
Are pages in that book, to show
How God Himself is found.

The glorious sky embracing all
Is like the Maker's love,
Wherewith encompass'd, great and small
In peace and order move.

The Moon above, the Church below,
A wondrous race they run,
But all their radiance, all their glow,
Each borrows of its Sun.

John Keble

There's a Friend for little children
Above the bright blue sky,
A Friend Who never changes,
Whose love will never die;
Our earthly friends may fail us,
And change with changing years,
This Friend is always worthy
Of that dear Name He bears.

Albert Midlane

As with gladness men of old
Did the guiding star behold,
As with joy they hail'd its light,
Leading onward, beaming bright;
So, most gracious Lord, may we
Evermore be led to Thee.

In the Heavenly country bright
Need they no created light;
Thou its Light, its Joy, its Crown,
Thou its Sun which goes not down;
There for ever may we sing
Alleluias to our King.

William Chatterton Dix

All people that on earth do dwell,
Sing to the Lord with cheerful voice;
Him serve with fear, His praise forth tell,
Come ye before Him and rejoice.

William Kethe

❦

Heaven gives our years of fading strength
Indemnifyng fleetness;
And those of youth, a seeming length,
Proportion'd to their sweetness.

Thomas Campbell

❦

And we shall see the plan sublime
Of his beneficent intent.
Live on in hope!
Press on in faith!
Love conquers all things,
Even death.

John Oxenham

When Nature tries her finest touch,
Weaving her vernal wreath,
Mark ye, how close she veils her round,
Not to be traced by sight or sound,
Nor soil'd by ruder breath?

Who ever saw the earliest rose
First open her sweet breast?
Or, when the summer sun goes down,
The first soft star in evening's crown
Light up her gleaming crest?

Fondly we seek the dawning bloom
On features wan and fair, —
The gazing eye no change can trace,
But look away a little space,
Then turn, and lo! 'tis there.

But there's a sweeter flower than e'er
Blush'd on the rosy spray—
A brighter star, a richer bloom
Than e'er did western heaven illume
At close of summer day.

'Tis Love, the last best gift of Heaven;
Love, gentle, holy, pure;
But tenderer than a dove's soft eye,
The searching sun, the open sky,
She never could endure.

The gracious Dove, that brought from Heaven

The earnest of our bliss,
Of many a chosen witness telling,
On many a happy vision dwelling,
Sings not a note of this.

So, truest image of the Christ,
Old Israel's long-lost son,
What time, with sweet forgiving cheer,
He call'd his conscious brethren near,
Would weep with them alone.

John Keble

I have no answer for myself and thee,
Save that I learned beside my mother's knee;
'All is of God that is, and is to be;
And God is good.' Let this suffice us still,
Resting in childlike trust upon His will
Who moves to His great ends unthwarted by the ill.

John Greenleaf Whittier

But now at thirty years my hair is grey—
(I wonder what it will be like at forty?
I thought of a peruke the other day—)
My heart is not much greener; and, in short, I
Have squandered my whole summer while 'twas May,
And feed no more the spirit to retort; I
Have spent my life, both interest and principal,
And deem not, what I deemed. my soul invincible.

What are the hopes of man? Old Egypt's King
Cheops erected the first Pyramid
And largest, thinking it was just the thing
To keep his memory whole, and mummy hid;
But somebody or other rummaging,
Burglariously broke his coffin's lid:
Let not a monument give you or me hopes,
Since not a pinch of dust remains of Cheops.

But I, being fond of true philosophy,
Say very often to myself, 'Alas!
All things that have been born were born to die,
And flesh (which Death mows down to hay) is grass;
You've passed your youth not so unpleasantly,
And if you had it o'er again—'twould pass—
So thank your stars that matters are no worse,
And read your Bible, sir, and mind your purse.'

George Gordon, Lord Byron

Riches I hold in light esteem,
And Love I laugh to scorn;
And lust of Fame was but a dream
That vanished with the morn—

And if I pray, the only prayer
That moves my lips for me
Is—'Leave the heart that now I bear,
And give me liberty.'

Yes, as my swift days near their goal,
'Tis all that I implore—
Through life and death, a chainless soul,
With courage to endure!

Emily Bronte

Thus deeply drinking in the soul of things
We shall be wise perforce; and, while inspired
By choice, and conscious that the Will is free,
Shall move unswerving – even as if impelled
By strict necessity – along the path
Of Order and of Good.

William Wordsworth

The snow has left the cottage top;
The thatch moss grows in brighter green;
And eaves in quick succession drop,
Where grinning icicles have been,
Pit-patting with a pleasant noise
In tubs set by the cottage-door;
While ducks and geese, with happy joys,
Plunge in the yard-pond brimming o'er.

The sun peeps through the window-pane;
Which children mark with laughing eye,
And in the wet street steal again
To tell each other spring is nigh;
Then, as young hope the past recalls,
In playing groups they often draw,
To build beside the sunny walls,
Their spring-time huts of sticks and straw.

The sunbeams on the hedges lie,
The south wind murmurs summer-soft;
The maids hang out white clothes to dry
Around the elder-skirted croft:
A calm of pleasures listens round,
And almost whispers winter by;
While Fancy dreams of summer's sound,
And quiet rapture fills the eye.

John Clare